"Christians Maturing into Leadership"

Jeff Mullins

Jeff Mullins

Copyright © 2020 Jeff Mullins

All rights reserved.

ISBN- 9798622624384

Cover Photo by Jeff Mullins: A guide leading a climber toward the summit of
"Monkey Face" at Smith Rock State Park, Redmond, Oregon

Table of Contents

INTRODUCTION...4

1 - It's about Time You are a Teacher...........................6

2 - Leadership Texts and Their Purposes....................14

3 - Understanding Leadership Titles and Terms...........21

4 - Leader Self Evaluation - Part 1.............................27

5 - Leader Self Evaluation – Part 2.............................33

6 - Evaluation by Others - Part 1...............................41

7 - Evaluation by Others – Part 2...............................47

8 - An Evaluation of Existing Leaders.........................51

9 – Other Selected Leadership Texts..........................56

ABOUT THE AUTHOR..62

Scripture Reference Index..63

INTRODUCTION

Jesus described discipleship with these words:

> *"A pupil is not above his teacher; but everyone, after he has been fully trained, will be like his teacher."* (Luke 6:40)

Becoming like Jesus is God's design for all disciples. New believers grow. They are just starting to down the road to become like Jesus. Mature believers, including leaders in the church, have been progressed some distance down the road of growth. Leaders help less mature believers grow to be like Jesus. As a leader in the church Paul was not shy to say:

> *"Be imitators of me, just as I also am of Christ."* (1 Cor. 11:1)

The New Testament identifies the qualifications/traits church leaders are to possess that demonstrate a spiritual maturity which is like Christ.

Every true follower of Jesus should be maturing toward possessing the same character qualities required of church leaders. Leaders are followers of Jesus who have progressed further down the path of spiritual maturity. Each and every Christian walks on the same path. Leaders are just further down the road. The goal for everyone is to be like Jesus.

Each Christian is a person saved by the grace of God to glorify God by becoming like Jesus. The new birth results in a new life. New life is characterized by spiritual growth. Growing toward spiritual maturity is normal for every Christian. Facilitating and encouraging this growth to the glory of God is the purpose of the church and the function of church leaders.

This book challenges all Christians to be growing into leadership. The Bible's teachings about the qualities and qualifications for church leaders are not just for leaders. These qualities describe the spiritual maturity that is the goal for every Christian. Every

Christian who is growing to be like Jesus is growing toward leadership.

Although it is clear that not everyone will hold a position of leadership in the church it is equally clear that every Christian should be purposefully growing toward becoming like Jesus and becoming qualified to be a leader. A Christian's failure to embrace growing to be like Jesus is to deny God's purpose and calling in salvation.

1 - It's about Time You are a Teacher
Hebrews 5:12

Take a few moments and thoughtfully answer the following questions.

Are you a Christian?

Are you a disciple of Jesus?

How long have you been a Christian?

After this time are you a teacher in the church? If not, then why not?

Are you qualified to be a teacher in the church? If not, then why not?

Are you a leader in the church? If not, then why not?

Are you qualified to be a leader in the church? If not, then why not?

<u>Me, a Teacher</u>?

How would you respond if someone approached you and asserted, "You have been a Christian for a while now, it is well past time you become a leader and teacher in the church."

If you are like many Christians you might resist the suggestion that you should be a teacher or a leader of some kind in the church. You may assert that you do not have the gift of teaching. Also, you may feel woefully inadequate and unqualified to be a church leader. After all, you might point out, a church leader has to have all areas of his life together, and it is obvious to everyone that you don't. Right?

Perhaps that is how the recipients of the book of Hebrews felt when they read these words:

> *For though **by this time you ought to be teachers,** you have need again for someone to teach you the elementary principles of the oracles of God, and you have come to need milk and not solid food. For everyone who partakes only of milk is not accustomed to the word of righteousness, for he is an infant. But solid food is for the mature, who because of practice have their senses trained to discern good and evil.* Hebrews 5:12-14 (emphasis added)

A few things are apparent from this text. The author of Hebrews  expected that eventually, at some time after a person became a follower of Jesus, they would be a teacher. Yet, the readers were not teachers. They were spiritually immature. They were unable to grasp spiritual truth. They could not discern good and evil because their senses were not trained. The writer also strongly suggests that if they were mature they would be teachers.

There are important questions that beg for answers in these verses. Why are these people immature? Who is to blame? Was it church leaders who failed to bring these people to maturity? Who, among all the people in the church, are these people that should be teachers? Is the expectation limited to those with a particular gift, the gift of teaching perhaps? Or, is this exhortation directed only to those called to a position of church leadership?

The writer to the Hebrews clearly lays the responsibility to become spiritually mature on each individual Christian. Although church leaders certainly have a role in bringing people to maturity[1], this text is reproving immature believers for their immaturity. They should, "by this time," be mature. They should "by this time," be teachers.

---

[1] Ephesians 4:11-13 asserts that God gave leaders to the church to equip the saints for spiritual maturity.

How should the writer's clear implication that each believer should be spiritually mature, and be a teacher, be understood? The answer lies in two things: 1) understanding what it means to be a disciple of Jesus[2], and 2) distinguishing the position of leadership from the function of leaders.

<u>Understanding Disciples</u>

Disciple is a familiar word. A disciple can be broadly defined as a follower or student of a teacher, leader, or philosopher.[3] This definition is generic but is  also consistent with the use of the term disciple in the Bible. Disciple is not so much a title as it is a description of what a person does. A disciple looks up to, learns from, follows after, mimics, and becomes like his teacher. A claim to be a disciple is only valid to the extent that the disciple follows and becomes like his master.

 A Christian is a disciple of a specific kind - a disciple of Christ (CHRIST-tian). Jesus Christ is the teacher from whom the disciple learns. Jesus is the leader whom the disciples follow. Jesus is the master to whom the disciple submits. The disciple of Jesus becomes like Jesus. Jesus Himself made this aspect of being a disciple very clear.

A disciple is not above his teacher, nor a slave above his master. It is enough for the disciple that he becomes like his teacher, and the slave like his master. . . (Matthew 10:24-25)

The goal of all disciples of Jesus is to become like Jesus. The Bible refers to the process of the disciple

---

[2] The author's book "<u>A Biblical Disciple</u>" examines some of the basic elements of salvation and what it means to be a follower of Jesus.

[3] Google search definition

becoming like Jesus as spiritual growth. The process of spiritual growth is sometimes also called sanctification which means to become separate or holy. Sanctification refers to the process involved in becoming more and more like Jesus. The more one grows to be like Jesus the more one is spiritually mature, or sanctified. The mature disciple will be holy, set apart and different from others because he has become like Jesus in substantial ways.

To claim to be a disciple of Jesus and to not be growing to be like Jesus is nonsensical. The essence of all discipleship is becoming like the master. This is what it means to be a follower of Jesus.

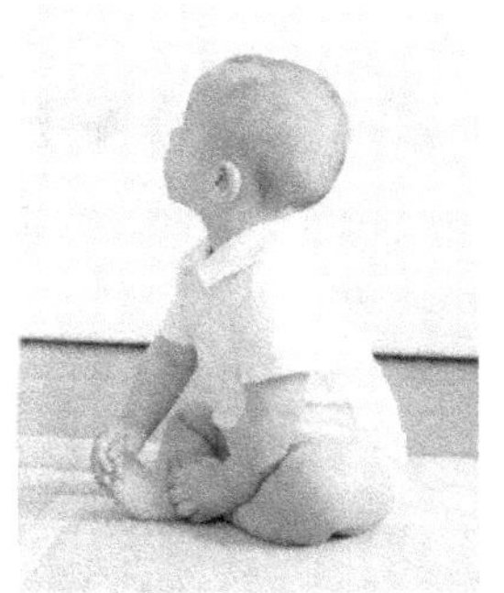

Sadly, it seems many people are content to take the designation "disciple" without making much, if any, progress toward being like Jesus. Nor do they seem to care if they mature or not. It appears this was perhaps the case with those to whom the writer to the Hebrews was directing his reproof in Hebrews 5:12. They were still immature. Enough time had elapsed that they should be mature. By now they should have been teaching others.

Growing into a mature Christ-likeness should be normal, not the exception. Every Christian is to be maturing into the likeness of Jesus.[4] It follows that, like Jesus, His disciples would do what He did – make disciples.

One pertinent text is familiar to most church going people:

> *And Jesus came up and spoke to them, saying, all authority has been given to Me in heaven and on earth. Go therefore and make disciples of all the nations, baptizing them in the name of the Father and the Son and the Holy Spirit, teaching them to observe all that I commanded you; and lo, I am with you always, even to the end of the age.* (Matthew 28:18-20)

---

[4]   Three chapters in "A Biblical Disciple" are devoted to identifying and explaining the ways the follower of Jesus is to become like Jesus.

This text is commonly called "The Great Commission." It is viewed by many as marching orders for the first disciples of Jesus as well as for subsequent disciples of Jesus. These verses are also often identified as the purpose and the "Mandate for the Church."

These designations may give the impression that making disciples is merely a task to be accomplished - a job to be done. Instead, making  disciples should be the normal result of being like Jesus. Boys and girls grow into men and women who get married and have children. That is normal just like making disciples is normal for the disciple who is truly a follower of Jesus.

True, there is the command in Matthew 28:19 to make disciples. Yet, do you think that Jesus made disciples because He was commanded? The answer to why Jesus made disciples comes in many forms. Jesus made disciples because He wanted to. Jesus wanted to do the will of His Father and to accomplish the work of the Father. He wanted to glorify the Father. Jesus did all that was needed to make disciples because He loved people.

For Jesus, making disciples was not just obeying a command, fulfilling a commission, or accomplishing a mandate. For Jesus, making disciples arose from His person, from His character, and from His nature. It was the result of His love for the Father and His love for people. 

It is the same love for the Father and love for people that should move the disciple of Jesus to do what Jesus did – make disciples. From that perspective the text at the end of Matthew 28 should be viewed as mostly a description of what the disciples of Jesus do. It could be stated this way:

Disciples of Jesus make Disciples: It is neither complicated nor hard to understand. The disciple of Jesus grows to be like Jesus. A person who is like Jesus will make disciples. To make a disciple one must teach. Every disciple must be a teacher. It is not necessarily a teacher with a title nor a position nor even one who is recognized as a teacher. A disciple is a learner, but also a teacher.

God's design for the church of Jesus is simple – more mature disciples lead, teach, and nurture less mature disciples. Individuals identified as leaders are not on a higher spiritual plane than others. Teachers and leaders are not super saints living a life unattainable by other disciples. No. They are just followers of Jesus that are a bit farther down the road of maturity in becoming like Jesus, and are leading others to follow Jesus.

Leaders – Distinguishing Function from Form

Recognized leaders in the church often are given titles like Pastor, Elder, Deacon, Trustee, or some variation of these. They typically hold identified positions of authority in the church and are usually looked up to as those who have a level of spiritual maturity. All of this is appropriate.

Yet, underlying each title a church leader is given there is a descriptive function that is to be accomplished by every follower of Jesus. To some extent at least, every disciple is to be functioning according to those descriptive titles. The more mature the disciple, the more they will function in the way the leader's title describes.

Consider the titles and the function that is to be fulfilled by every disciple.

A **Teacher** is one who communicates the truth of God to others – something every disciple should do.

A **Leader/Elder/Overseer/Bishop** is one who is looked up to as an example to be emulated and followed – something every disciple should do.

A **Pastor/Shepherd** cares for God's people, feeding, protecting, and guarding them – something every disciple should do.

A **Deacon/Minister** is one who serves others – something every disciple should do.

A **Trustee** is one who is trustworthy and faithful – something every disciple should do.

A **Reverend** is one who has reverence and respect toward God – something every disciple should do.

Each title describes a character quality or service that should be part of every disciple's life. The more spiritually mature the disciple is, the more these attributes will be present. The titles are the form leadership takes, but the function described by the title is to be increasingly true of each and every disciple, position or not.

Most will readily admit that leaders are to be followed. For the disciple of Jesus, church leaders should be an example to follow for becoming more like Jesus. This perspective was clearly held by the apostle Paul when he wrote to the saints in Corinth, *"Be imitators of me, just as I also am of Christ."* (1 Corinthians 11:1) Paul was not some super saint. He was a disciple of Jesus who was just a bit further down the road of spiritual maturity.

Each disciple of Jesus is expected to be progressing along that road of spiritual maturity. Before them are those whom they can follow to become more like Jesus.

Behind them are those who are following them, looking to them as an example of following Jesus.

Most may never hold a position of leadership nor be given a title in the church. But there should be no doubt that every disciple of Jesus is to fulfill the function of pastor/shepherd, teacher, and leader because they are growing to be like Jesus who is the good shepherd, the faithful teacher, and the true leader.

When the writer to the Hebrews asserts that, "by this time you ought to be teachers" he is speaking of spiritual maturity. Spiritual maturity is being like Jesus who made disciples because of His love for the Father and His love for people. The mature disciple makes disciples for the same reasons.

When you hear the words, "by this time you ought to be teachers," how do you respond?

The bottom line is that every disciple of Jesus should be maturing toward leadership. Not necessarily the position of leadership, but certainly the function of leadership.

This book is about all believers progressing along the path of spiritual maturity. As the Bible's qualifications, traits, and requirements for leaders are considered, you will be encouraged to grow and to mature personally as a disciple of Jesus. By looking at what the Bible says about leaders, each Christian is given practical help in understanding what their life should be.

2 - Leadership Texts and Their Purposes

Church leaders are to be examples of what it looks like to be like Jesus. They are selected as leaders because their lives consistently demonstrate a high level of spiritual maturity. Each believer should be able to see the character of Jesus in their leaders. Each Christian should be able to become more like Jesus by following their leaders' examples. As the church leader follows Jesus he provides a tangible flesh and blood example on earth of what it looks like to follow Jesus.

Contrary to what many seem to think, church leaders do not have a higher standard to live by than any other believer.[5] All believers, including leaders, are to be like Jesus. Leaders are individuals formally recognized as having grown to be like Jesus to an extent that enables them to be a consistent example for others. They are still human. They are not perfect. However, they are further down the road to maturity than most.

Those selected for leadership positions in the church must have a significant degree of spiritual maturity to be a Christ-like example. To ensure leaders are mature, God has provided clear and specific criteria for the evaluation and selection of church leaders. The criteria for leaders are primarily character traits that Jesus possessed. They are traits that each follower of Jesus should increasingly possess. Thus each disciple should personally embrace leadership criteria as what God desires for each Christian.

---

[5] To be sure, leaders have more accountability because of their position, but that should not be confused with having a different standard for how to live; All Christians are to grow to be like Jesus.

The New Testament texts describing qualifications for church leaders fall into three broad categories.

- Some texts describe criteria for <u>self evaluation</u> by one aspiring to leadership.

- Other texts describe criteria <u>existing leaders</u> are to use for evaluating someone who is aspiring to leadership.

- A third type of text describes criteria to be used to evaluate the ongoing ministry of <u>those already in leadership</u>.

The New Testament also has sections that give instructions, or describe the work of church leaders, that are not directly describing the qualifications of leaders.

The texts describing the qualification of church leaders have different purposes. Understanding these different purposes[6] is very important.

Each type of text will be introduced in this chapter and considered in more detail later.

Text Describing Self Evaluation

One Bible text is focused on self evaluation prior to aspiring for a leadership position.

Church leaders are commonly called Pastor, Preacher, Minister, Elder, Bishop, Overseer, etc. The Bible uses all of these terms. Some titles are used frequently, other rarely. Pastor is the least used term in the New Testament for a leader, yet in many circles it is the most common

---

[6] Good Sermon Brother, Jeff Mullins, Create Space Independent Publishing Platform (June 29, 2013) explains the principles of interpretation and the importance of identifying both the meaning of a text and its purpose.

title.[7] On the other hand, Teacher is a title scarcely used as a title for a leader in the church. Yet, Teacher (or Rabbi) is used in the Bible a number of times as a title for a leader, especially by Jesus.

James uses the title Teacher to describe church leaders in chapter 3 of his book. It is clear from the text that James uses the word Teacher as a title for a leadership position. Consider the reasons why it should be understood that the term teacher in James 3:1 should be viewed as a leadership title and position.

- All disciples function as teachers as they engage in discipleship.[8] The intent of the text is certainly not intended to discourage or prevent "discipleship-type" of teaching.

- All who teach are accountable for what they teach. The church leader falls under "greater judgment" and accountability than other disciples because of his position and influence.

- James includes himself as a Teacher when he says "we shall incur a greater judgment." James was a leader in the Jerusalem church.

- The book of James was possibly one of the earliest New Testament books written[9] When the church first began, and when James wrote, the church was primarily Jewish believers. The Jews commonly used the terms Elder and Teacher to refer to their leaders.

- Jesus referred to His role and position as Teacher.

For theses reasons it seems clear that James is referring to the <u>position</u> of Teacher/Leader, not just the <u>function</u> of teaching. Although the teaching of James 3 applies to all followers of Jesus, it is directly addressed and most applicable to those considering a leadership position.

James instructs those who are thinking about aspiring to a position of Teacher/Leader to approach it with seriousness. Each one was to evaluate himself regarding his spiritual maturity. Before pursuing an position of

---

[7] There are good reasons why churches refer to their leaders as Pastor. The reasons will be discussed later in this book.

[8] Matthew 28:20 . . . making disciples includes "teaching them to observe all that I commanded you.

[9] Some date James before AD50 (John MacArthur study Bible for example)

leadership a self evaluation must be taken and passed. Two specific areas that indicate spiritual maturity are to be evaluated: 1) Self-control as evidenced by control of one's tongue and 2) possessing wisdom from God.

He who lacks self control is warned not to seek a position as a Teacher/Leader. He who lacks God's wisdom is warned not to seek a position as a Teacher/Leader. Becoming a Teacher/Leader without possessing the required maturity will bring God's judgment.

A second type of text describes how existing leaders are to assess potential leaders.

<u>Texts Describing Evaluation **BY** Existing Leaders</u>

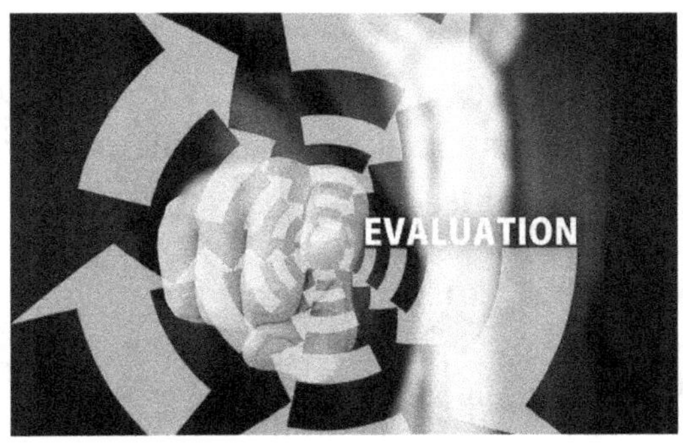

After self evaluation aspiring leaders are to be assessed by the existing leaders. Existing leaders are assumed to have spiritual maturity needed to identify what is important and to discern the maturity level of the leadership candidate.

In his letters to Titus and Timothy Paul told them (existing leaders) to evaluate and appoint other leaders in the churches. The criteria for assessing potential leaders are explained in these texts[10]. Before being appointed to leadership existing leaders were to verify that aspiring leaders possessed spiritual maturity evidenced by being above reproach in all areas of their lives.

Before becoming a leader, each man is to be assessed first by himself and then by existing leaders. After a man is placed in leadership there are other criteria by which his ministry is to be evaluated. Like many things

---

[10]   1 Timothy 3:1-13 and Titus 1:5-9

in life, the criteria for assessing job performance are different than the entry requirements.

<u>Text for Assessing Existing Leaders</u>

Peter, in 1 Peter 5:1-4, addresses his instructions to "the elders among you," as a fellow elder. He puts himself in the same category as those to whom he writes, an elder.

He identifies the priority of elders is to shepherd (pastor) the flock of God in a way that provides an example for the flock. The leader is to be a humble steward who serves for the well being of God's people, not for personal gain.

Although the texts in James, 1 Timothy, and Titus remain relevant to some extent, it is this text in 1 Peter 5 that should provide the primary basis for evaluating the ongoing ministry of leaders in the church.

Also, it is clear from this text that a variety of terms or titles are associated with the same position/role of church leaders[11]. Peter gives these instructions to <u>elders</u>[12], the word used among Jews as a title for a leader. He commands the <u>elders</u> to shepherd the flock of God and uses the verb form of the word for <u>pastor</u>[13]. He tells them to provide oversight, the verb form of the word often translated bishop or <u>overseer</u>[14]. This is a word used by the Romans to refer to leaders.

The leader in the church functions as a shepherd for God's people as an example while holding a position that may be identified by a number of different titles.

---

[11]   There is a similar use of these terms by Paul in his address to the leaders from Ephesus as recorded in Acts 20.

[12]   The Greek word is presbuteros

[13]   The Greek word is poimain

[14]   (The Greek word is episkopos)

Insight From Other Texts

The evaluation and assessment of leaders at the different stages and times should rest primarily upon the applicable texts mentioned above according to the specific purposes(s) for which each is intended.

However, there are also other significant texts that contribute to the understanding of the character, roles, and functioning of leaders in the church. Included in the short lists of texts would be the entire books of 1 Timothy, 2 Timothy, and Titus as well as Acts 20:17-35. These texts contain specific instructions to existing church leaders regarding their work.

Also, there are texts that provide insight into the life and ministry of the Apostles and church leaders as examples to follow. The most obvious texts of this type are those describing the work, ministry, and character of the Apostle Paul.

Sometimes individuals whose lives are described in the Bible such as David, Nehemiah, Ezra, Moses, etc are held up as examples of leadership. While these may provide some examples of leadership, their lives also are examples of blatant failure in leadership at times. These narrative texts may provide some illustrations of leadership, but they should not be considered as the primary instructions of what leaders should be or do. For the church, and for Christians, the Lord Jesus is the example and definition of a leader. The church leaders and all disciples are to be like Jesus.

Follow the Leader

Leaders in the church are examples to be followed as they follow Jesus. Leaders are selected and serve, not as super saints, but as those with some level of maturity to lead others into maturity.

All disciples of Jesus should be growing to be like Jesus. Leaders in the church provide an example of what it looks like to be a bit further down the road to maturity.

The following chapters describe the specifics of what God says leaders should be. By considering these specifics each disciple gains insight into what spiritual maturity looks like. Each Christian is to be maturing into Christ which is also maturing into leadership as they grow in the character traits that leaders should possess.

3 - Understanding Leadership Titles and Terms
1 Timothy 3:1-13

It is important to understand the similarities and differences between the terms and titles used for leaders in the church. As previously noted, each term refers to a function as well as a title for leaders. Although not every Christian will hold the office of a leader, each Christian should possess, and be growing in, all of the functions that all the various titles suggest. This is because each term also is directly related to the character of Jesus. Understanding the meanings of the different terms helps each follower of Jesus to grow to be like Jesus.

Leader – is a generic and broad term referring to one who provides guidance, direction, oversight, and an example. Inherent in the term disciple, and in the process of discipleship, is the distinction that one is a leader and the other is a follower. One is the teacher, teaching the other who is a learner. One is setting the example; the other is following the example. These functions are to be accomplished by those in positions of leadership to be sure. However, leading is something every disciple of Jesus is to be doing as well. Each disciple is following. Each disciple is leading others.

Elder – refers primarily to being of an older age, senior. Often, by implication, elder implies there is wisdom that the experience of years produces. In many cultures the term elder is applied as a title, formal and informal, specifically to older individuals that possess such wisdom. These elders are looked to with respect and their counsel is often sought out. Frequently the one recognized as holding a position of Elder possessed some authority that others are expected to follow.

The leaders among the Jews, the heads of families and clans, were called elders. Leaders in the Jewish social/political structure were also called elders as evidenced throughout the Bible.

Likewise, in the church which arose out of Judaism and the Jewish synagogues, the term elder was naturally adopted to refer to those who were recognized as leaders. The church in its early days consisted mostly of Jews[15] and church leaders were naturally called elders.

Not surprisingly, the term elder occurs scores of times in the Bible in both the Old Testament and New Testament. When the term elder is found in the Bible the context reveals whether it is speaking of Jewish elders or leaders in the church of Jesus Christ – church elders. Significantly, the term elder most often occurs in the plural.

The elders were those with experience, wisdom, and maturity; sometimes they were recognized as such and given the title, Elder.

All followers of Jesus are growing in experience, wisdom, and maturity. As they mature, they become an example for others and a resource for wisdom and insight into how to live a life pleasing to God. All believers, to some degree, can and should function as elders, whether they have a position or title or not.

Bishop/Overseer – is the term used in the Greek/Roman world instead of elder. While elder perhaps had a more family/clan flavor, overseer was more of a supervisory or political title. The word literally means one who watches over, having responsibility for, and oversight of, some particular realm.

Similar to how the Jewish term elder was adopted into the church, so too the Greek/Roman term for leader, overseer, came to be applied to the

---

[15]   The book of Acts records that the spread of the gospel to the Gentiles did not occur in significant measure until the rise of persecution of the church. Only then did there become a significant numbers of Gentiles in the church.

church leadership positions. The word overseer only occurs a handful of times in the Bible as the title for a church leader. Sometimes the word is translated bishop.

<u>Pastor</u> - means shepherd. Pastor is a title used in protestant churches perhaps more frequently than any other term to refer to the most prominent leaders in churches. There are pastors, senior pastors, youth pastors, associate pastors, music pastors, etc. Yet the word pastor/shepherd is seldom used[16] in the most commonly used translations of the Bible to refer to church leaders.

This disparity between the number of times the Bible uses the word and its prolific use in modern churches is because Pastor is more a function than a title. No matter what the title of the church leader may be, he is a shepherd of the flock. His job is shepherding, caring for, guarding, protecting, feeding, nourishing, and healing the flock.

The picture of a shepherd caring for his flock is prominent at many different levels in the Bible. The leaders and kings of Israel are called the shepherds of God's people (Ezekiel 34). Jesus is the Good Shepherd (John 10:1-18) and He is the Great Shepherd (Hebrews 13:20). Of course, the Lord is the shepherd (Psalm 23). The Messiah was to be the LORD Himself who would come and shepherd His people Israel and would feed His flock (Ezekiel 34:11-24).

When Jesus appeared to the disciples, as recorded in John 21, He commanded Peter to care for His sheep. Three times, in response to Jesus' question about Peter's love for Him, Jesus told Peter "tend My lambs," "shepherd My sheep," and "tend My sheep." No matter what

---

[16] The only place pastor(s) is found in the NASB is Ephesians 4:11 And He gave some as apostles, and some as prophets, and some as evangelists, and some as pastors and teachers,

Peter said in response to Jesus' questions, Jesus told Peter to do the work of a shepherd – to take care of Jesus' sheep. The sheep are the people in the church.

Church leaders may have different titles, but their function is always shepherding/pastoring God's flock regardless of what they are called. This fact is made very clear in two New Testament texts referring to the singular office of leader but use the terms interchangeably.

Peter, in his instructions to church leaders in 1 Peter 5:1-4, addresses his instructions to "elders." He commands these with the title of elder, to "shepherd/pastor" God's flock. As they shepherd, they are exercising "oversight" which is the word for overseer/bishop. Elder is the title. Shepherding is the function. Overseeing the flock is part of shepherding. Peter refers to himself as a fellow elder and refers to God/Jesus as the Chief Shepherd to whom all leaders are accountable. The flock belongs to God.

Similarly Paul makes it clear in the account recorded in Acts 20:17-38 that elders and overseer/bishops are the same office of which the function is shepherding. Paul calls for the "elders" of the church (20:17), saying the Holy Spirit made them "overseers" (20:28) while identifying that their function is to "shepherd" the church of God.

It is appropriate that the leaders in the church be called Pastor, since that word best describes their function as a caring, nurturing shepherd of the flock.

However, the function of shepherding is not unique to those who are given a title of leadership. Caring for, protecting, feeding, reproving, warning, etc, is the function of every Christian. Every follower of Jesus is to be connected to other followers of Jesus in discipleship relationships where shepherding is occurring. Christian parents are to shepherd their children, husbands shepherd their wives, Sunday School teachers shepherd their students, and youth leaders shepherd the youth. The function of pastoring is a common responsibility for each Christian in all their relationships. It is not about having authority, title, or position. Pastoring is about loving and caring for people so they might know Jesus and grow into Him.

Every follower of Jesus, the Great Shepherd and the Good Shepherd, is to be growing to be like Jesus. The person who grows to be like Jesus will be a shepherd to others. This is the natural outcome of spiritual growth. Being a pastor is not just a position in the church or a title, it is the nature of a follower of Jesus.

<u>Deacon-Minister</u> is a servant. The distinction is often made that deacons address physical and material needs among the flock while elders are responsible for

meeting spiritual needs. This perspective is partly based on Acts 6:2 which records the 12 apostles saying "It is not desirable for us to neglect the word of God in order to serve tables." Seven men were chosen to serve in the distribution of food. Although the word deacon is not used in this text, the function of serving certainly is present.

However, all christians are to be servants in function. Jesus said that the greatest of all is the servant of all.[17] Jesus set the example of being a servant ultimately in laying down His life for the salvation of mankind.[18] Similarly, every Christian is to be a servant as they follow Jesus.

The titles given to church leaders all have underlying functions. These functions are to become part of the character of every follower of Jesus. As disciples grow to have the character of Jesus they become disciple makers like Jesus. As such they lead others, they care for others like a pastor, they are an example, and they serve others. These are all things associated with spiritual growth and maturity.

---

[17] Matthew 23:11
[18] Philippians 2:5-8

Every disciple of Jesus should be growing in these things and therefore maturing into leadership. The titles for leaders in the church illustrate what all Christians should be.

4 - Leader Self Evaluation - Part 1
James 3:2-13 Self Control

Let not many of you become teachers, my brethren, knowing that as such we will incur a stricter judgment. James 3:1

It has already been observed that the word teacher in this verse is referring to being a leader in the church, not just functioning as one who teaches. Certainly, the text is applicable to all Christians. However, the primary focus and most direct application is to those thinking about becoming leaders in the church.

This text is specifically speaking about the position of being a Teacher/Leader, not just about someone accomplishing the function of teaching. It is clear that each disciple following Jesus will be involved in teaching in informal ways as a minimum as a disciple. The expectation put forth in Hebrews 5:13 is that after some period of time each person would be a teacher, able to teach others.

There is a warning here. Being a leader in the church is a weighty responsibility for which there is a greater level of accountability. Leadership is a position of prominence, visibility, and greater influence. People are influenced by those they look 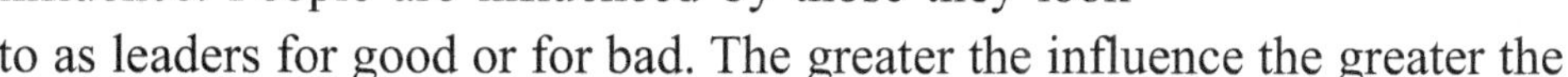

to as leaders for good or for bad. The greater the influence the greater the

judgment. The immature person can be a bad example which may lead others to stumble into sin. It is quite foolish to seek to be a leader when you lack the required maturity.

The warning is not intended merely to dissuade a person from seeking a leadership position. Rather it is a caution that each person should carefully evaluate himself <u>before</u> aspiring to a position of leadership. One should first honestly evaluate their own spiritual maturity before seeking to be put into leadership.

Aspiring to be like Jesus is a good thing. Aspiring to leadership is a good thing if the motives are right and it is the result of being like Jesus. This is affirmed when Paul writes to Timothy "It is a trustworthy statement: if any man aspires to the office of overseer, it is a fine work he desires *to do*." 1 Timothy 3:1

The warning in James 3:1 is that to be a leader one must possess and demonstrate a level of spiritual maturity so he does not stumble and does not cause those who follow him to stumble. Ironically, one of the characteristics of immaturity is over estimating maturity in one's self. The evidence of maturity, James asserts, is found in two areas of life: self-control and demonstrating wisdom from God.

<u>Self Control</u>

The mature follower of Jesus possesses self control. Self control is epecially evidenced by the words one speaks, how one speaks, and when one speaks; James calls this the tongue. The perfect man is one who does not stumble in what he says. If he is able to control what he says, he is able to control his whole body as well.

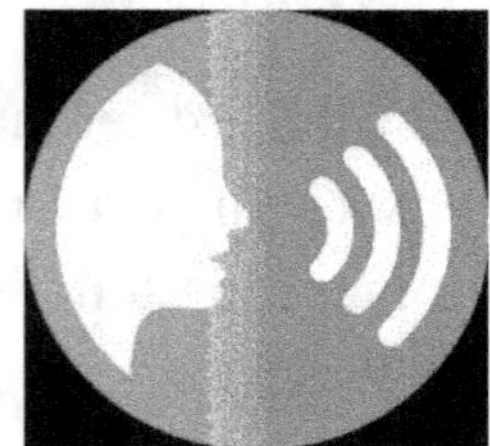

The issue is not the tongue alone. The issue is whether or not a person is mature. Having a self control that keeps one from stumbling in what he says indicates overall spiritual maturity, being "perfect."

No one should get hung up on the use of the word perfect. Being perfect indicates a completion or a level of accomplishment that is appropriate. James has already used this term in chapter one regarding the outcome of trials.

Consider it all joy, my brethren, when you encounter various trials, knowing that the testing of your faith produces endurance. And let endurance have its perfect result, so that you may be <u>perfect and complete, lacking in nothing</u>. James 1:2-4 (Emphasis added)

Spiritual growth and maturity is the result of having a proper attitude in trials. The goal of God for the trials in the life of His children is perfection, maturity. Paul uses the same word to describe the goal of his ministry in the individuals he serves.

We proclaim Him (Jesus), *admonishing every man and teaching every man with all wisdom, so that we may present every man complete <u>(perfect)</u> in Christ.* Colossians 1:28 (Emphasis added)

Everyone understands that no one, other than Jesus, is perfect in the absolute sense. Church leaders are not perfect. However, leaders are to have a level of completeness and maturity that enable them to be a Christ like example. That maturity is, James says, evidenced in self-control in one's speech.

Self-control of the tongue is an indicator that one has self-control in all areas.

For we all stumble in many ways. If anyone does not stumble in what he says, he is a perfect man, able to bridle the whole body as well. James 3:2

The issue is not just the words one says. The focus is on the heart of the man that enables him to control his tongue. Jesus said that it is what comes out of a man's mouth that indicates what is in his heart.

But the things that proceed out of the mouth come from the heart, and those defile the man. For out of the heart come evil thoughts, murders, adulteries, fornications, thefts, false witness, slanders. These are the things which defile the man . . . Matthew 15:18-20

When there has been a heart change, then there will be changes in what one says. Self-control is not simply about words, but about the heart that gives rise to the words.

The change of heart is accomplished by the Holy Spirit. When a person is  controlled by the Spirit and walking in the Spirit they will demonstrate the fruit of the Spirit which includes self-control[19].

James' point is that <u>before aspiring</u> to be a Leader each person should assess whether or not they are spiritually mature as evidenced by self-control of the tongue. James goes on to give several illustration of how powerful and significant control of the tongue is.

He points out that small things control large things: a bit in a horse's mouth controls the horse; a small rudder controls a great ship in powerful winds; a small fire like a single match sets a whole forest aflame.

The one who can control their tongue has self control over their whole body.

---

19 Galatians 5:22-23 But the fruit of the Spirit is love, joy, peace, patience, kindness, goodness, faithfulness, gentleness, **self-control**; against such things there is no law.

So also the tongue is a small part of the body, and yet it boasts of great things. See how great a forest is set aflame by such a small fire! And the tongue is a fire, the very world of iniquity; the tongue is set among our members as that which defiles the entire body, and sets on fire the course of our life, and is set on fire by hell. James 3:5-6

James also highlights that the tongue ranks as the most challenging and difficult thing to contain among all the things in the world to be controlled.

For every species of beasts and birds, of reptiles and creatures of the sea, is tamed and has been tamed by the human race. But no one can tame the tongue; it is a restless evil and full of deadly poison. James 3:7-8

God can change the heart and the tongue. The man who has self control over his tongue demonstrates that God has produced maturity in his life. James also focuses on consistency in self-control. The tongue that is only sometimes controlled is a tongue that is not under control.

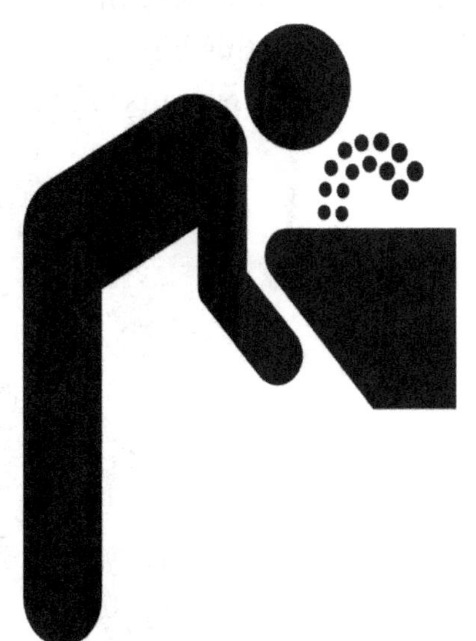

With it we bless our Lord and Father, and with it we curse men, who have been made in the likeness of God; from the same mouth come both blessing and cursing. My brethren, these things ought not to be this way. Does a fountain send out from the same opening both fresh and bitter water? Can a fig tree, my brethren, produce olives, or a vine produce figs? Nor can salt water produce fresh. James 3:9-12

It is common for most people to have control over their speech at some times and in some circumstances. Employees bite their tongue until they are out of earshot of the boss. Church going people manage usually to avoid swearing and angry outbursts while at church. Parents don't typically yell and threaten their children when in public but when the setting changes, many people flap their tongue without restraint. This limited restraint is not the type of self-control that indicates spiritual maturity. What is in the heart eventually comes out.

Spiritual maturity befitting those aspiring to church leadership comes from a heart of self-control that puts forth a consistent pattern of speech under all circumstances. This level of self-control is evidence that God has changed the heart perspectives and attitudes in the life of a person.

Self-control is not just for the church leader, or aspiring church leader. Self-control is the fruit of the Spirit of God that God desires in the life of every one of His children. Jesus demonstrated self-control in His words and actions because of what was in His heart. As the follower of Jesus becomes more and more like Jesus, he will demonstrate this kind of self-control. As a disciple of Jesus matures to be like Jesus he is maturing into leadership.

5 - Leader Self Evaluation – Part 2
James 3:13-18 Wisdom

After tasking the aspiring leader to do a careful self assessment of the level of self-control in his life, James put forth a second criteria - possessing and demonstrating God's wisdom.

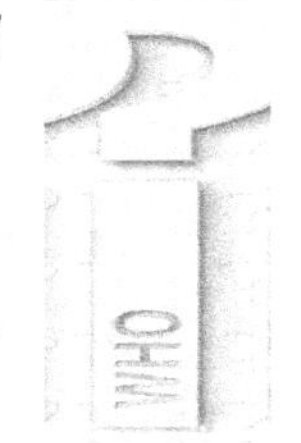

James 3:13 asks, *"Who among you is wise and understanding?" Then it says, "Let him show . . ."*

This is a functional continuation of how James chapter 3 begins, *"Let not many of you become teachers* 3:13 introduces the next criteria by asking . . . *who among you is wise and understanding?"*

Both sections begin by asking "who?" Who has self-control? Who is wise and understanding?

The self assessment of the aspiring church leader includes evaluating whether he possesses the wisdom of God. James clearly identifies that not all wisdom is wisdom from God. Also he makes it clear what the wisdom of God is like.

Also, it is insufficient to claim to have wisdom without demonstrating wisdom in action. The command in James 3:13 is "let him show" that he is wise and understanding.

Although it may never be verbalized, most people think they are wise and understanding. Most people, especially those who are immature, are prideful over estimating what they are really like. Thinking you are wise is quite different from actually being wise. The claim to be wise is required to be validated with concrete evidence in life. It must be shown.

James 3:13 puts it this way *". . . let him show by his good behavior his deeds in the gentleness of wisdom."*

It is the deeds that a person does that shows that he is wise and understanding, not just his words alone. These are the actions, the works, and the attitudes in his life. Of course deeds include what he says and how he says it.

Deeds show wisdom "by his good behavior." The deeds are the individual actions. The good behavior is the general course and direction of the life. Like a convict whose sentence is reduced, good behavior is not the presence or absence of any particular actions. Rather, good behavior is the characterization of the whole life. The wise person does specific good deeds, but also has a life that is seen by all as being characterized as good.

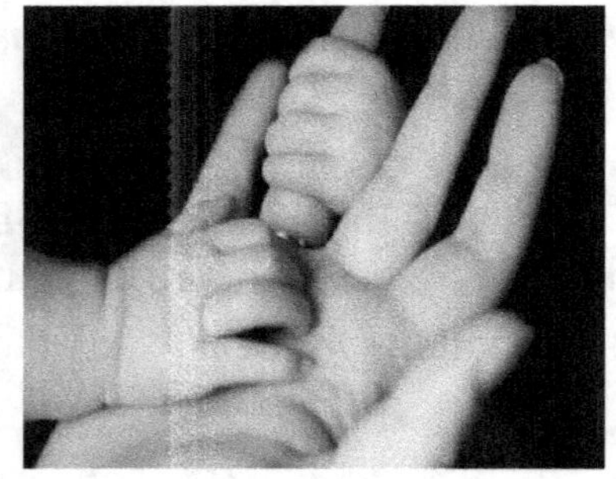

The life and deeds of wisdom are further identified as being done "in the gentleness" of wisdom. Wisdom is not just about what is done, but how things are done. The clear implication is that if a person lacks gentleness in their life or in their deeds, that person lacks wisdom. Gentleness, like self-control, is a trait identified in Galatians 5:23 as being the fruit of the Spirit. The person who walks by the Spirit demonstrates the fruit of the Spirit including self-control and gentleness.

The one aspiring to leadership is not left on his own to define the type of wisdom required. James identifies that there are two types of wisdom and each has easily identifiable traits. There is the wisdom of the world and there is the wisdom of God. Only the one who possesses the wisdom of God should consider himself as eligible for a position of leadership in the church.

Wisdom NOT from God

The remaining verses in the text describe and contrast wisdom from God with wisdom that is not from God. First the wisdom not from God is described:

"But if you have bitter jealousy and selfish ambition in your heart, do not be arrogant and so lie against the truth. This wisdom is not that which comes down from above, but is earthly, natural, demonic. For where jealousy and selfish ambition exist, there is disorder and every evil thing." James 3:14-16

To claim to have God's wisdom when your life does not demonstrate it is to lie against the truth in arrogance. It is pride that claims to possess God's wisdom when it is not present.

Two characteristics are said to not arise from the wisdom of God and both of them may be present in someone aspiring to leadership. The individual is challenged to reflect on whether or not there is bitter jealousy or selfish ambition in his heart in wanting to be a leader.

Bitter jealousy could be wanting to be a leader because of dissatisfaction or resentment toward others, perhaps particularly toward other leaders. Selfish ambition is desiring to step up into leadership because of the potential benefits which you may enjoy. These traits indicate a spiritual immaturity and a lack of understanding of the importance of submission and service in the life of a leader.

This is the one who selfishly aspires to leadership wanting to get recognition and praise for personal gain. This is the one who loves to be first, and to be seen as first.

Earthly wisdom views leadership as a competition with others. Being the leader is seen as a higher position with power or control over other people. The earthly-wise man views ascending to a position of leadership as a victory over others. This type of wisdom comes naturally to sinful people and is characteristic of the fallen world.

Self centered earthly wisdom leads to disorder and every evil thing (James 3:16). This is not the type of wisdom that is to be put on display as an example that disciples of Jesus should be encouraged to follow.

The one with this natural wisdom should not be so arrogant to say that he is wise and understanding. The one who is guided by worldly wisdom does not have God's wisdom. When one

recognizes worldly wisdom in himself it should postpone aspirations for leadership in the church. It is arrogant, and contrary to the truth, to claim to be wise, when the wisdom governing the life is not of God.

The selfishness, arrogance, and jealousy of earthly wisdom are evidence of spiritual immaturity. The spiritually immature person should not aspire to leadership. Instead, they should devote themselves to growing into the likeness of Jesus. Possessing the world's wisdom and God's wisdom are mutually exclusive.

The wisdom from God is called wisdom from above. It does not come naturally from within a person. It is not found in the world around a person. God's wisdom comes only from God.

Instead of originating from God's wisdom, arrogance, selfish ambition, and jealousy come from being earthly, natural, demonic. Earthly wisdom is consistent with the world, It is in contrast to wisdom from heaven/God. Natural wisdom comes from our nature which is selfish and self serving. Demonic wisdom is consistent with the Devil who is a liar and deceiver and opposed to God's purposes. Wisdom of the world, the flesh, and the devil is not from God.

Wisdom FROM God

God's wisdom is in contrast to earthly wisdom. God's wisdom eliminates selfish ambition. It excludes bitter jealousy. God's wisdom leads to promoting 

order. It produces good deeds. If a life is filled with chaos and disorder it certainly is not governed by God's wisdom.

Having highlighted the characteristics of earthly wisdom, James then describes God's wisdom in terms of the life of one governed by it.

> *But the wisdom from above is first pure, then peaceable, gentle, reasonable, full of mercy and good fruits, unwavering, without hypocrisy. And the seed whose fruit is righteousness is sown in peace by those who make peace.* James 3:17-18

Although there are many traits listed in these verses, there are three major segments or divisions in the sentences that describe God's wisdom. Not every trait is given equal emphasis. God's wisdom is <u>first</u> pure, <u>then</u> (a list of grouped traits) <u>and</u> (a description of the outcome).

"First!" God's wisdom is pure. The word means clean, innocent, and modest.[20] The use of this word seems to reflect on both the personal purity of the individual and also on the purity of motives. There is no selfishness nor jealousy in the wisdom from above. Instead, there is a love for God and a love for people that seeks leadership in order to be able to most effectively serve. The first and foremost impact of possessing wisdom from above is the unnatural change in the heart of the individual. Their life and motives are pure not self-centered.

"Then!" Next comes a list of traits that are loosely connected as all being relational. ". . . *peaceable, gentle, reasonable, full of mercy and good fruits, unwavering, without hypocrisy . . .*" Wisdom from above first changes the heart on the inside and then it changes how one relates to people. The wisdom from above results in a person being genuine, easy to get along with, and truly caring about other people.

"And!" The outcome is peace.

> *And the fruit of righteousness is sown in peace by those who make peace.* James 3:18 (author's translation[21])

Fruit refers to what is produced, the outcome. The phrase "the fruit of righteousness" refers to the righteousness that comes through God's wisdom. The

wisdom of God produces a righteous life. The outcome of righteous life

---

[20] Thayer's Greek Definitions
[21] This is a literal rendering of the Greek text as translated by the author.

is attitudes and actions that plant seeds in the lives of others in peace. The one with God's wisdom is one who makes peace.

Gentleness and peace are prominent traits in this text describing the

wisdom of God. The question ask is, who is the one who is wise and understanding? The answer is the one who demonstrates gentleness and peace in their life. As noted earlier, the traits possessed by one who is wise and understanding are consistent with the fruit of the Spirit demonstrated in the life of one who is walking by the Spirit: (. . . *love, joy, **peace**, patience, **kindness**, goodness, faithfulness, **gentleness**, **self-control** . . .*" (Galatians 5:22-23 emphasis added)

James 3 is most directly applicable to those aspiring to a leadership position – *"Let not many of you become Teachers/Leaders."* However, each and every Christian is to be growing into the maturity of leadership. Gaining wisdom from above is growing in Christ-like maturity, the goal for each follower of Jesus.

In salvation God, by His grace, gives to each of His children the perfect positional righteousness of Jesus. Spiritual growth is the process where each person becomes more and more like Jesus, more and more righteous in their practice.

James 3:13-18 explains that spiritual maturity can be measured in relative amounts of earthly wisdom and God's

wisdom. The immature disciple is controlled much by natural wisdom and little by God's wisdom. The mature follower of Jesus is controlled mostly by God's wisdom and little by earthly wisdom.

James instructs him who aspires to leadership positions to take an honest look at what kind of wisdom governs his life. The leader is an example to be followed by God's people. He must demonstrate God's wisdom so others may grow to be more and more controlled by the wisdom of God.

Leaders are not on a higher plain. They are just a bit further down the road of wisdom, God's wisdom. This self evaluation of those aspiring to leadership is a self evaluation that should be a routine part of every believer's life.

6 - Evaluation by Others - Part 1
1 Timothy 3:1

1 Timothy is a letter from the Apostle Paul to provide instructions to Timothy who is a leader in the church. One important function of leaders in the church is appointing other men to positions of leadership after evaluation.

The assumption is that existing church leaders have spiritual maturity and God's wisdom. For this reason they are tasked with evaluating others who are aspiring to leadership. Selection of leaders is not left up to the congregation which likely consist of a mix of mature and immature believers as well as possibly even some

unbelievers.[22] According to the Bible, leaders are not elected through democratic processes. Leader selection is to be based upon spiritual criteria as assessed by those who have a proven history of spiritual maturity, existing leaders.

The spiritual criteria specified for leaders are not marks of super saints. They are simply characteristics that accompany the spiritual maturity that all followers of Jesus should be growing toward.

---

[22] Although leaders are not evaluated or selected by the people in the congregation, their level of spiritual maturity should be apparent to all. Part of the process should include gathering input from people in the congregation as part of the evaluation of aspiring leaders.

The spiritual criteria for evaluating leaders provide a basis for every Christian to evaluate himself and to work toward.

Assessing Leadership Aspirations

Although it is not normally highlighted as an important leadership qualification, the motive one has in reaching out toward leadership is a vital and potentially disqualifying factor.

> *"Faithful the word: If someone is aspiring of becoming overseer, he is desiring a good work."* 1 Timothy 3:1 (author's translation[23])

The focus is on the **work** of the overseer. The focus is not the office, position, or title. The "good thing" of being a leader is the **work** that the position of church leader has associated with it. Aspirations for leadership should arise from desiring to do the work of the leader, not just wanting the position. Someone may have strong aspirations for a leadership position, but if he does not desire the work, he is not qualified. Additionally, any motivation other than a desire to do the work disqualifies the aspiring leader from the position.

In the church people often aspire for leadership positions for the same reasons people in the world aspire for leadership. They may want power, fame, respect, honor, money, or influence. They may want to be the boss. They may want to rule over others. They may want to tell others what to do rather than having someone telling them what to do.

Jesus made this distinction in attitude and motives very clear by how He response to two of his disciples seeking status over others.

> *But Jesus called them to Himself and said, "You know that the rulers of the Gentiles lord it over*

---

[23] This is a literal rendering of the Greek text as translated by the author.

them, and their great men exercise authority over them. It is not this way among you, but whoever wishes to become great among you shall be your servant, and whoever wishes to be first among you shall be your slave; just as the Son of Man did not come to be served, but to serve, and to give His life a ransom for many. Matthew 20:25-28

According to Jesus, aspiring to leadership is seeking to become a servant in order to do the work of a servant. Seeking leadership should have nothing to do with what the leader gets from holding the position. Being a leader is about the opportunities it provides to serve and the benefit netted by those served.

The concept of serving others seems to be increasingly uncommon in our world where serving self and advancing self is prevalent and promoted as good. To some extent, at least in previous times, it was common for doctors, teachers, pastors, and perhaps even some public office holders to choose their life's work to help people. This is rare today. Many, if not most, choose their life's work with little or no consideration of how they will benefit any but themselves and their own. Many view parenting in the same self centered way; that somehow being a parent is about meeting their personal needs, wants, or desires for self fulfillment. Similarly, many wrongly view and seek leadership in the church as something that is a benefit to the leader. Christian leadership is to be sought as a means of benefiting those who are led, not for the benefit to the leader.

The work of the overseer is shepherding. That is what the word pastor means. Pastoring (shepherding) is caring for people so that they come to know Jesus as their Savior and to grow to be like Him. Shepherding is discipleship. Shepherding is a mature follower of Jesus discipling another disciple of Jesus. Shepherding is hard work.

The one aspiring to a leadership position should already be doing the work of discipleship/shepherding. Aspiring to leadership is seeking increased opportunities to disciple and shepherd.

Leadership: More Discipleship Opportunities

Individuals who hold positions or titles of leadership within the church have a status that invites others to look to them for spiritual help. The one aspiring to be a leader is desiring increased opportunity to do the work of a shepherd. When one is identified as a leader, there is a significant increase in the opportunities to help others that comes with the position and title.

If someone has a question about the Bible, they ask the pastor, or Bible teacher, or someone identified as a leader. If one needs spiritual advice or counseling, they will seek out the identified leader. When there is to be a wedding, or funeral, or a hospital visit, people call the pastor. If mediation is needed in conflict or if a sin needs to be confronted, people look to the identified leaders.

When seeking spiritual help in big or small issues people naturally look to the identified leaders. Absent the identification as a leader the opportunities to serve are often more limited. Someone who is qualified to be a leader, but not identified as a leader, will normally have fewer opportunities to serve than the one holding a leadership position. Admittedly there are opportunities to serve in the church without being a

leader. Yet the leader, by token of being identified as such, has more opportunities.

Additionally, the leader in the church often has more opportunity to serve because the church is obligated to meet the leaders' physical and material needs to free him up for spiritual concerns.

Although there is a warning that aspiring leaders not be motivated by money, it is proper that the aspiring leader expect compensation for his spiritual service. This expectation is proper when it is not motivated by the money itself, but because there are greater opportunities to serve when material needs are adequately met.

It is for this same reason that mature Christian's seek financial stability in their lives. The wise use of financial resources frees people to serve. Contentment with modest material means frees people to serve. Freedom from financial debt frees people to serve. In the same way, one who is appointed to leadership may have financial support that frees him to serve. It is the freedom and opportunity to serve that is sought, not the financial support alone.

With spiritual growth there is an increasing desire to serve other people. Although many will never hold a position of leadership, the desire to serve others is something that every follower of Jesus should possess and have increasing in their lives.

The first step of existing leaders evaluating potential leaders is to determine if their motive is to do the work of a leader. Are they committed to glorifying God by doing the work of making disciples or do they have some other motive?

*"Faithful the word: If someone is aspiring of becoming overseer, he is **desiring a good work**."*

1 Timothy 3:1 (author's translation)

GOOD
WORK

7 - Evaluation by Others – Part 2
1 Timothy 3:2-13[24]

Every Christian is to be growing into maturity so that they become like Jesus. Leaders are those who have a recognized level of maturity that provides an example for other followers of Jesus. The criteria for evaluating leaders is the same criteria each disciple should strive to grow into so that God will be glorified in their lives.

The evaluation of potential leaders by existing leaders looks at the same basic areas as the self evaluation as discussed in the previous chapters. The self evaluation assessed spiritual maturity as evidenced by self-control and demonstrating God's wisdom. Self-control is ultimately displayed in the ability to control the tongue. Wisdom is demonstrated in a life characterized by gentleness and peace among other things. The evaluation by existing leaders looks for the practical outworking of these character traits in every area of the potential leader's life.

There is a small, but important, detail in the wording of 1 Timothy 3:2, "An overseer **then** must be above reproach." A completely literal translation of this text is "It is necessary **therefore** the overseer above reproach to be." The words "then" and "therefore" reflect back to verse 1 which says that it is a good/valuable work he desires. The assessing of spiritual maturity, and the associated character qualities, therefore focus on whether or not he is capable of doing the work. For many may desire to do the work but because of some lack they are not capable to do the work.

---

[24] Many books have been written that examine this text in minute detail. This book simply looks at the big picture of the qualifications they relate to spiritual maturity that should be normal goals for all followers of Jesus.

1 Timothy 3:1-13 first provides the criteria first for assessing overseers, and then for assessing deacons. Although overseers are generally responsible for spiritual care and deacons focus more on physical/material matters, the qualifications are basically the same. Apart from slight variations, both overseers and deacons are required to meet the same high standard of spiritual maturity, they are to be above reproach.

3:2 "*An <u>overseer</u>, then, must be above reproach, . . .*"

3:10 "*. . . let them serve as <u>deacons</u> if they are beyond reproach . . .*"

To be above reproach is to be blameless. It is to be above accusation that is legitimate. It is not being absolutely perfect. It is having a life that consistently demonstrates the traits of spiritual maturity. Although it may

be thought that there is a long list of criteria in this text, there is only one, being above reproach. For leaders to accomplish their functions people must have respect for them. Being above reproach is having a life that is worthy of the respect the position requires.

Time is required to grow into maturity and time is also needed to confirm that spiritual maturity exists.

3:6 overseers must be ". . . *not a new convert, . . .*"

3:10 deacons ". . . *must also first be tested; then let them serve as deacons if they are beyond reproach.*"

Even if a recently saved person seems to be above reproach, and seems to demonstrate spiritual maturity, he is not to be placed into leadership until time passes. An immature person is prone to pride that will hamper effective leadership. As time passes a person's true character becomes evident as he is observed in service and when facing life's various challenges. A person qualified for leadership will have a heart for service and already be serving in many ways without having any official position.

All Christians are to be growing toward becoming above reproach, like Jesus. The specifics of Christian character that evidence being mature and above reproach can be loosely grouped into broad categories of attitudes, relationships, and abilities.

Specifically, the mature person's relationship with his spouse, children in the home, other household members, and those outside of the church is orderly, under control and well managed. His life is well controlled and without excesses in any area including money and alcohol. He is kind, gentle, and patient being able to avoid contention and needless conflict. His reputation merits respect and enables him to communicate his grasp of God's truth so that people will be willing to listen. He is seasoned in God's grace and not prone to having an overinflated view of himself.

For leaders, all of these "qualifications" are essential for them being able to accomplish the work of caring for God's people.

The parallel text in Titus 1 emphasizes many of the same things. An implied requirement for leadership in 1 Timothy is clearly stated in Titus. The leader must be

*". . . holding fast the faithful word which is in accordance with the teaching, **so that he will be able** both to exhort in sound doctrine and to refute those who contradict."* (Titus 1:9 emphasis added)

Spiritual maturity always includes understanding and living consistently with God's Word. This is an essential element of a leader's life that makes him able to carry out the work of a leader, discipleship. Making disciples includes exhortation/encouragement in sound teaching and being able to point out false teachings when they occur.

In all these things leaders are Christians who are mature. They are not super saints. They do not have a higher standard than any other Christian. All Christians are growing to be like Jesus, and therefore growing into leadership.

The criteria given for the evaluation of potential leaders provide a helpful picture of some of the practical aspects of spiritual maturity and what it looks like to be like Jesus.

8 - An Evaluation of Existing Leaders
1 Peter 5:1-5

Previous chapters have considered the marks of spiritual maturity to be assessed in consideration of someone becoming a leader (elder) in the church of Jesus Christ. James 3 contains self evaluation criteria. 1 Timothy 3 and Titus 1 provides guidance for existing leaders to use to evaluate potential leaders. Another text, 1 Peter 5:1-8, puts forth the considerations to be used to evaluate those who are already serving as leaders.[25]

The function of the leader is revealed in the command "shepherd the flock of God." Caring for God's people as a shepherd is the task of the leader - feeding, guarding, encouraging, and correcting as needed.

Although a leader has the authority from Christ to lead God's flock, he does not lead from a position of superiority or pride. This text emphasizes that just as the flock belongs to God, so does the shepherd-leader who is tasked with leading them. As recorded in John chapter 21, three times Jesus asked Peter if he loved Him. No matter what Peter answered, Jesus commanded him to tend, feed, care for (shepherd) My sheep. Making disciples, and serving as a church leader, is shepherding people.

Peter the Apostle identifies himself as a fellow elder, even though he walked with Jesus, saw His glory on the mountain, and was an eye

---

[25]   Although the other texts provide a measurement of maturity applicable to all Christians, including existing leaders, 1 Peter 5:1-8 is the primary criteria for evaluating the ongoing ministry of leaders in the church.

witness of the death and resurrection of Jesus. He puts himself on the same level as the elders to whom he is writing.

Note that three words are used in the text to refer to the church leaders. All three terms refer to the same person. <u>Elder</u> is the title used to refer to the leaders. <u>Shepherd (pastor)</u> is the term that describes the leaders function. The phrase "exercising oversight" is the word that is associated with the title <u>overseer/bishop</u>. By referring to himself as a fellow elder, and using these three terms to refer to the leadership position, Peter dismisses the idea of a hierarchy in church leadership.

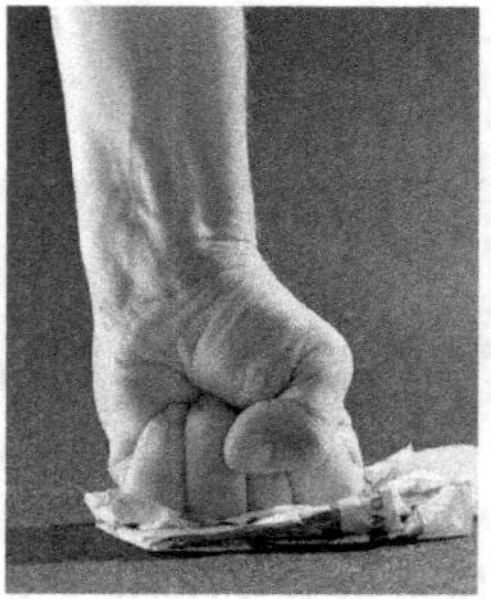

Similarly, the shepherd is not to domineer or run roughshod over people as if he were different or better than they. Leaders are to humbly serve God's people being an example. As mature believers who are a bit further down the road leaders show those following them how to love, care, and have concern for other people.

The mature Christian serves the Lord by serving people because that is what he wants to do. He volunteers to serve. He serves from the heart not feeling that he is being compelled to serve.[26]

Similarly, the leader is not in it for the money. Although God commands His people to provide materially and financially for their leaders, the leader has a heart that is eager to serve whether he is paid or not. Material provision simply frees him up to serve more.

---

[26] The compulsion in view here is that the man leads because he needs a job, because someone expects it of him, because he needs the money, etc. It is right an appropriate to have an inner compulsion to serve because the love of God compels the service.

Neither is it the earthly benefits, perks, or rewards of serving the Lord that motivates the mature Christian to faithfully serve. Service is humbly rendered with a focus on the recognition and reward for service that justly comes to those who have served well. The Chief Shepherd (Jesus) will appropriately compensate each of his servants when He appears. This perspective enables the servants of God to continue in faithfulness during times of great difficulties.

In each of the previous texts it has been made very clear that pride is an indicator of spiritual immaturity. Pride, which shows itself in many ways, disqualifies a man from leadership positions. James chapter 3 linked arrogance and selfish ambition with the perspective and attitude of the world and its wisdom. Paul, in 1 Timothy 3 warned that a new Christian should not be appointed to leadership lest he become snared by pride. Pride is an overinflated view of self. Humility is an accurate view of self that enables relating to people with compassion and empathy rather than with superiority and harshness that pride produces.

The text in 1 Peter 5 affirms that pride has no place in leadership in the church.

"You younger men, likewise, be subject to your elders; and all of you, clothe yourselves with humility toward one another, for God is opposed to the proud, but gives grace to the humble."
1 Peter 5:5

Notice the word *"likewise."* Younger men are told to be in submission to their elders in the same way that elders are to be in submission. Elders are to humbly submit to the Chief Shepherd to set an example of submission that all can follow. God is opposed to those leaders who are proud. God is opposed to anyone who is proud. Pride is contrary to the truth and is therefore a perspective and attitude that is contrary to faith. Humility is seeing self, and others, consistent with faith in the truth.

Although leaders have a position, title, and authority, they are, along with every believer, commanded to *"clothe yourselves with humility toward one another."* There is a sense then in which leaders are to have the same humility of submission toward those whom they lead. This humble mutual submission is the result of being filled with the Spirit and is a mark of spiritual maturity.

> *". . . **but be filled with the Spirit**, speaking to one another in psalms and hymns and spiritual songs, singing and making melody with your heart to the Lord; always giving thanks for all things in the name of our Lord Jesus Christ to God, even the Father; **being subject to one another** in the fear of Christ."* (Ephesians 5:18-21 emphasis added)

Submission is an attitude of humility of the spiritually mature. Those who lead well must first be humble followers themselves. Humility ensures that the leader sees himself as being on the same plane, and having the same needs for God's grace, as those he leads. He does not view himself as elevated above or better than others. The leader is a humble follower of Jesus that is a bit further down the road than those he leads.

In the verses that follow (1 Peter 5:6-9) there is a command for the followers of Jesus to humble themselves. For those who don't there is a warning that the Devil is on the prowl to devour whomever he can. Taken in its context, and what is consistently taught throughout the scriptures, it is clear that those who are proud are more susceptible to falling into sin.

The humility of which Peter speaks underlies every aspect of how existing leaders are to be evaluated. Their attitudes, motives, priorities, and expectations are all formed by an accurate view of the truth about themselves and others – the very definition of humility.

Understanding the foundational importance of humility in spiritual maturity also provides some insight into the other texts that have been considered regarding those aspiring to leadership positions. The self-control and wisdom that James emphasizes in the self evaluation process are the results of humility. Pride discards the need for self control and elevates independent thinking over God's truth.

Similarly, when Paul tells Titus and Timothy that leaders must be above reproach he is telling them to see if humility is demonstrated in all areas of life. Reproach comes upon the life governed by pride.

The instructions Peter gives regarding evaluating existing leaders really comes down to whether or not the leader is demonstrating the attitudes, heart, and type of service that Jesus did. Is the leader like Jesus, humble? The leader who is like Jesus has the spiritual maturity that each and every follower of Jesus is to be growing into. The leader, like every follower is a work in progress.

Humility = Maturity = Above Reproach = Leader

9 – Other Selected Leadership Texts

This chapter considers lessons in spiritual maturity from a few selected texts that provide valuable insight and perspective on the qualifications and duties of leaders in the church.

The New Testament books written by Paul to Titus and Timothy are often referred to as the Pastoral Epistles, or letters to pastors. In these books the instructions from the apostle to men who are serving as leaders provide a wealth of information about the work of leaders and what spiritual maturity looks like. One text that is  particularly insightful into the work and perspective of the church leader is found in Paul's 2nd letter to Timothy written as Paul approached the end of his life.

But refuse foolish and ignorant speculations, knowing that they produce quarrels. The Lord's bond-servant must not be quarrelsome, but be kind to all, able to teach, patient when wronged, with gentleness correcting those who are in opposition, if perhaps God may grant them repentance leading to the knowledge of the truth, and they may come to their senses and escape from the snare of the devil, having been held captive by him to do his will. 2 Timothy 2:23-26

A dominate theme in 2 Timothy is the central role of God's Word in the work of the leader. The leader is to preach the Word (4:2), having diligently studied the Word (2:15), having been made adequate by the Word (3:16-17), and to pass on the Word to other faithful men (2:1-7).

Contrasting the emphasis on God's Word is a backdrop of those who neglect the Word of God and focus instead on speculations (2:23), engage in worldly and empty chatter (2:16), as well as those who are deceiving and being deceived (2:13), and those who turn away from the truth to myths (4:4).

The mature Christian is able to distinguish between clear truth of the scriptures and that which arises from men's imaginations. He purposefully does not "wrangle about words, which is useless and leads to the ruin of the hearers." (2:14) The mature Christian gives major emphasis to major issues, minor emphasis on minor issues, and altogether avoids engaging in discussions that have no certain answer in God's Word and only leads to quarrels. The mature Christian

must not be quarrelsome because it does not profit and is a stumbling block to those who need to hear the truth.

The mature Christian also understands that there are several different parties involved in a person repenting and coming to knowledge of the truth. The above text identifies the parties as the Lord's bond-servant, God, the individual, and the devil.

The Lord's bond-servant cannot save anyone, but he does have a role in their salvation. He is not to be quarrelsome, but instead teaches the truth in kindness, gentleness, and with patience. He is to confront error while demonstrating the fruit of the Spirit.

At the same time the Lord's bond-servant understands that the unrepentant person is held in the snare of the devil to do the devil's will and that God must grant him repentance. Although God is the One who grants repentance, it is the responsibility of the individual himself to come to knowledge of the truth and to repent. These dynamics are involved in evangelism and in the spiritual growth in people's lives.

Understanding the various roles, and the limited but vital role he personally plays, the Lord's bond-servant is humble and faithful even in the face of prolonged periods of opposition and times of seeming fruitless efforts. He is faithful in speaking the truth with gentleness, trusts in God to produce the growth, and urges people to repent and place their faith in God that they may be freed from their bondage. These characteristics are to be present and increasing in the life of every follower of Jesus. The leader demonstrates, models, and teaches by example how all believers should relate to others.

Another helpful text is found in the testimony of Paul and his instructions to the elders at Ephesus as recorded in Acts 20.

> " . . . *serving the Lord with all humility . . .   I did not shrink from declaring to you anything that was profitable,. . . testifying . . . of repentance toward God and faith in our Lord Jesus Christ. . . .   I have coveted no one's silver or gold or clothes. You yourselves know that these hands ministered to my own needs and to the men who were with me. In everything I showed you that by working hard in*

this manner you must help the weak and remember the words of the Lord Jesus, that He Himself said, 'It is more blessed to give than to receive.'" (Excerpts from Acts 20:19-35)

The servant heart of the mature Christian is seen in the leadership of Paul who lived out the truth that it is more blessed to give than to receive. Not only did he sacrificially preach the gospel in personal hardship, he worked hard to support himself and those with him. He was aware that every aspect of his life was an example. He purposed to make sure that his example was worthy of being followed and he encouraged others to follow it. Every disciple of Jesus should follow Jesus in such a way that we should be comfortable encouraging others to follow our example that they too might follow Jesus.

Although it may initially seem strange to be included in the discussion about maturing into leadership, Hebrews 13:17 contains some insight into the heart of a mature Christian and church leaders.

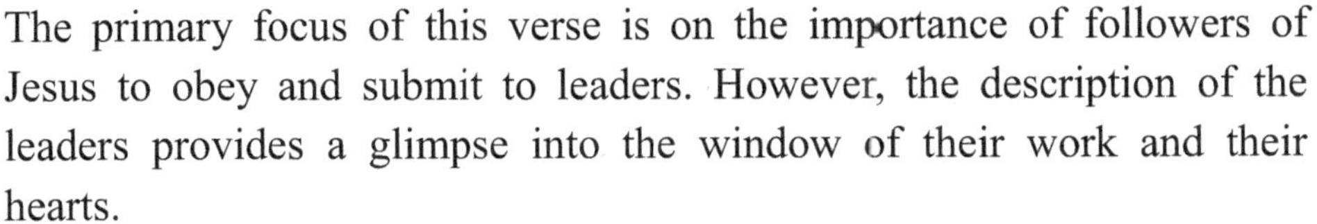

Obey your leaders and submit to them, for they keep watch over your souls as those who will give an account. Let them do this with joy and not with grief, for this would be unprofitable for you. (Hebrews 13:17)

The primary focus of this verse is on the importance of followers of Jesus to obey and submit to leaders. However, the description of the leaders provides a glimpse into the window of their work and their hearts.

Although leaders cannot save anyone, they carry a huge burden to watch out for those under their care. The mature Christian watches out for the spiritual well being of others, and leaders especially will have a reckoning before God as to how well they applied themselves to that work. The writer to the Hebrews brings the gravity of this task into the

light as a basis and motivation for the disciples to obey their leaders.

Additionally, leaders are exposed as truly caring for the Lord's people to such an extent that how the people obey either causes joy or grief. Like parents responding to their beloved children, faithfulness and obedience produces joy. On the other hand rebellion and disobedience cause a deep heartfelt sadness, grief. Of course where there is grief there is also need for corrective action, and thus he reminds them that a lack of obedience and submission would not be profitable for them. All followers of Jesus should rejoice in obedience and grieve over sin.

In the same way, Paul appeals to the believers in Philippi to "make his joy complete" by being unified in humility following the example of Christ.[27] Mature believers are willing to invest deeply into the lives of other people exposing themselves to potential grief and heartbreak when they stray from the truth. Never-the-less they faithfully serve with humility and love because they are following the example of Jesus.

Summary

Many think that church leaders are hybrid super saints on an elevated spiritual plane that is inaccessible to most people. It is also commonly thought that the requirements for church leadership exceed what is required of non-leaders. However, both of these ideas are false and display a lack of understanding of Christian leadership and the goal God has for every Christian.

---

[27] Philippians 2:1-10

Each Christian is to be growing to be like Jesus. The qualifications for leaders are simply measures of Christian maturity. Thus each Christian who is obeying God and working to becoming like Jesus is becoming increasingly qualified to become a leader in the church. Each Christian should embrace spiritual growth and strive for the leadership traits to the glory of God.

You may or may not become a leader in the church. However, it is God's clear design and purpose that grow to become like Jesus and thereby have the maturity that glorifies God by being worthy of leadership.

ABOUT THE AUTHOR

Jeff Mullins is a tent making pastor serving in rural churches in Northwestern Oregon for the past 25 years. During that time he has been actively involved in discipleship and training men. His ministry includes teaching others to carefully interpret the Bible and effectively preach. He has conducted pastoral training in Russia and Africa. He has work extensively discipling men with various addictions.

Jeff has a great passion for God's Word and a fervor for careful interpretation and purposeful practical application.

Jeff is a member of the IFCA International and has served as a missionary pastor with Northwest Independent Church Extension (NICE) and has been serving at Canaan Community Church in Deer Island, Oregon for over two decades.

Jeff is married to Mary Mullins since 1979 and they have seven children together, most of whom are actively involved in Christian service.

Jeff is the author of other books including:

> Dating and marriage: Avoiding Hell On Earth
> Children: Raising or Ruining?
> My Beloved Addiction: Finding True and Lasting Freedom
> You Can Understand the Bible
> A Biblical Disciple

Jeff operates a portable sawmill business Creation Woods (creationwoods.com) to support his family and to be able to contribute to missions work around the world. More information and resources can be found at canaanbiblechurch.com and jeffmullinsbooks.com.

All of Jeff's books are available at Amazon.com and many are in ebook format as well.

1 Corinthians 11:1...4, 12
1 Peter 5:1-4..18, 24
1 Peter 5:1-5..51
1 Peter 5:1-8..51
1 Peter 5:5..53
1 Peter 5:6-9..54
1 Timothy 3..51
1 Timothy 3:1..28, 41p., 46
1 Timothy 3:1-13..17, 21, 48
1 Timothy 3:10...48
1 Timothy 3:2...47p.
1 Timothy 3:2-13...47
1 Timothy 3:6..48
2 Timothy 2:1-7..57
2 Timothy 2:13...57
2 Timothy 2:14...57
2 Timothy 2:15...57
2 Timothy 2:16...57
2 Timothy 2:23...57
2 Timothy 2:23-26..56
2 Timothy 3:16-17..57
2 Timothy 4:2..57
2 Timothy 4:4..57
Acts 20:17-35..19
Acts 20:17-38..24
Acts 20:19-35..59
Acts 6:2...25
Colossians 1:28..29
Ephesians 4:11...23
Ephesians 4:11-13...7
Ephesians 5:18-21..54
Ezekiel 34...23
Ezekiel 34:11-24...23
Galatians 5:22-23..39
Galatians 5:23...34
Hebrews 13:17..59
Hebrews 13:20..23
Hebrews 5:12..6

Hebrews 5:12-14...7

Hebrews 5:12...9

Hebrews 5:13...27

James 1:2-4...29

James 3...51

James 3:1..27p.

James 3:13...33

James 3:13-18...33, 39

James 3:14-16...35

James 3:16...36

James 3:17-18...37

James 3:18...38

James 3:2...29

James 3:2-13...27

James 3:5-6...31

James 3:7-8...31

James 3:9-12...31

John 10:1-18...23

John 21..23

Luke 6:40..4

Matthew 10:24-25..8

Matthew 15:18-20...29

Matthew 20:25-28...43

Matthew 23:11...25

Matthew 28:18-20...9

Matthew 28:19...10

Matthew 28:20...16

Philippians 2:1-10...60

Philippians 2:5-8...25

Psalm 23..23

Titus 1...51

Titus 1:5-9...17

Titus 1:9..49